LIFE OF A HONEY BEE

A BOOK ABOUT THE LIFE CYCLE OF HONEY BEES

AMELIA LOCKHART

Acknowledgements:
Part of the content was adapted from the following sources.
Anon (n.d.). Honey bees. [online] honeybeenet.gsfc.nasa.gov. Available at:
https://honeybeenet.gsfc.nasa.gov/Honeybees.htm.
Anon (2010). The Honey Bee Life Cycle. [online] BuzzAboutBees.net. Available at:
https://www.buzzaboutbees.net/honey-bee-life-cycle.html.

Dictionary ©2022 Wordsmyth https://kids.wordsmyth.net/

Illustrations credited to Canva®

LIFE OF A HONEY BEE

A BOOK ABOUT THE LIFE CYCLE OF HONEY BEES

AMELIA LOCKHART

LIFE CYCLE OF A HONEY BEE

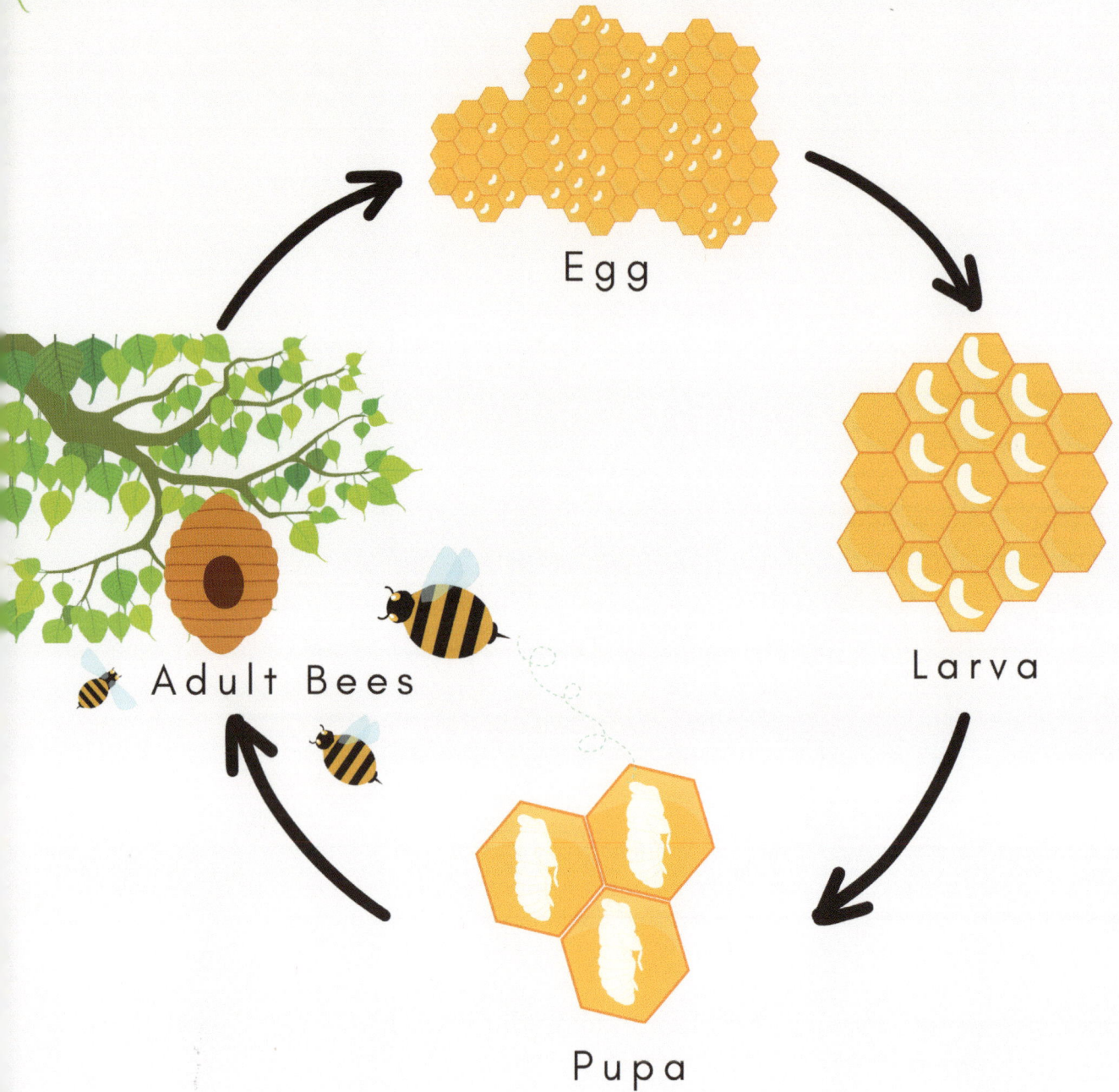

Egg

Larva

Pupa

Adult Bees

BEES HAVE 4 LIFE STAGES

1 Egg stage

2 Larva stage

3 Pupa stage

4 Adult bee stage

EGG STAGE

A queen bee lays her **eggs** on a honeycomb. The queen bee lays one egg on each cell of the honeycomb.

The queen lays two types of eggs. One type of eggs will become female honey bees and the other type of eggs will become male honey bees.

Female honey bees are called worker bees.
Male honey bees are called drones.

Did you know that a queen bee can lay thousands of eggs? A queen bee can lay between 2,000 to 3,000 eggs!

LARVA STAGE

After the eggs hatch, a tiny larva is born. The larva looks like a worm. It doesn't have legs, wings, or antenna.

The nurse bees feed the larva royal jelly. Only the bees that will become queens will be fed royal jelly throughout their life.
The bees that will become workers and drones will be fed pollen and honey.

Did you know that the queen bee is the largest bee in the **colony**?
The queen bee is the biggest bee in the hive.

PUPA STAGE

The larva forms a cocoon around itself, they are protected inside the cell which is covered by wax. Inside the cocoon the larva **transforms** into an adult honey bee. This change process is called **metamorphosis**.

ADULT HONEY BEE STAGE

After the metamorphosis is complete a fully grown honey bee will **emerge** from the honeycomb cell.

Did you know that honey bees are fed by the older bees for a few days before they begin to feed themselves?

How many honey bees can you spot?

PARTS OF A HONEY BEE

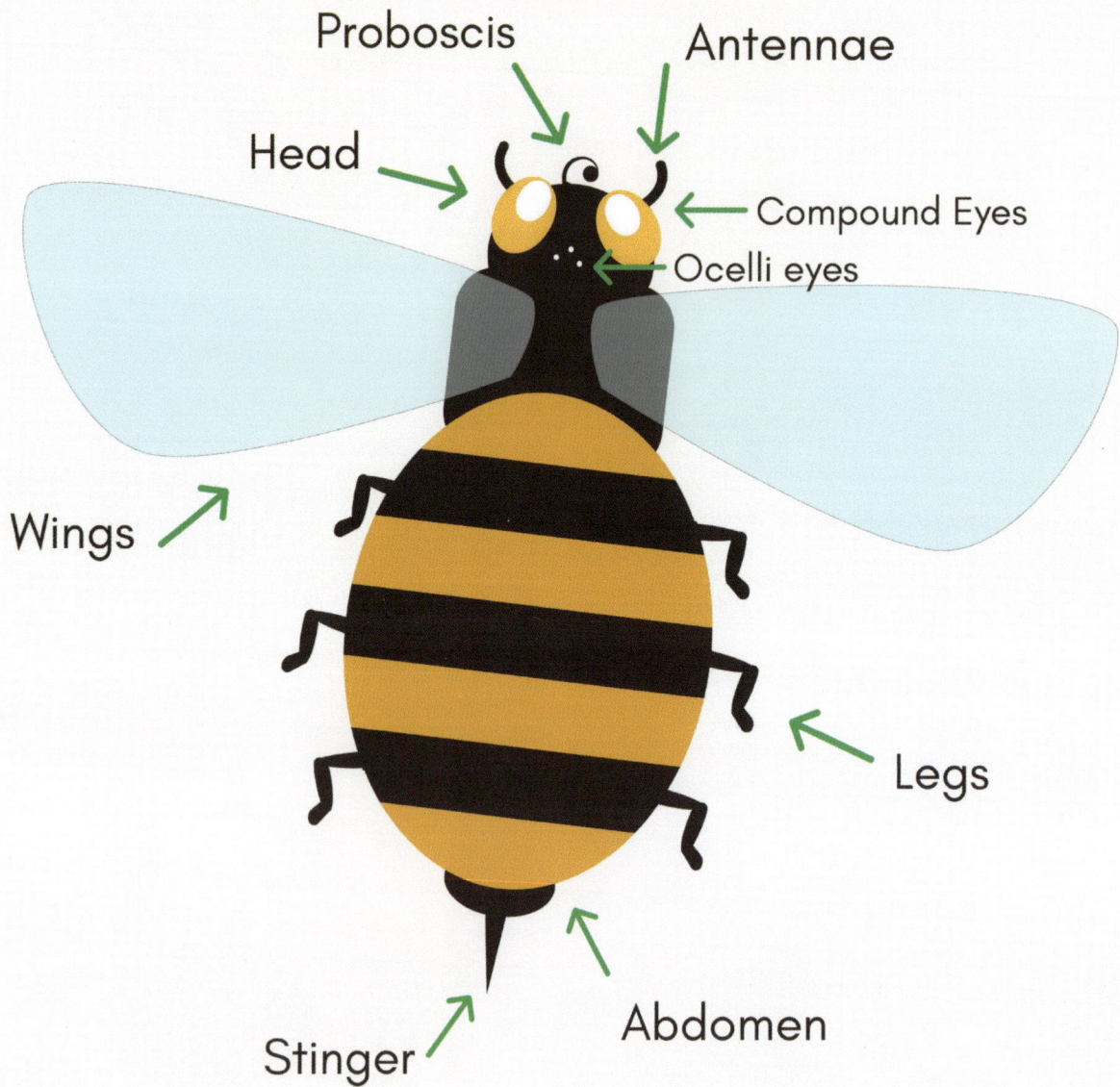

Proboscis

Antennae

Head

Compound Eyes

Ocelli eyes

Wings

Legs

Stinger

Abdomen

Head: In their head honey bees have a mouth, two compound eyes, ocelli eyes, two antennae and a proboscis.

Antennae: Honey bees use their antennae to smell flowers, food, and to feel animals or other things that are moving around them.

Eyes: Honey bees have two types of eyes. One pair of eyes are very special and are called **compound** eyes. It is like having many little eyes. This helps the bees see in many directions at the same time. They can see forwards, backwards, above and below all at the same time!
The other type of eyes are called **ocelli** eyes used to detect movement.

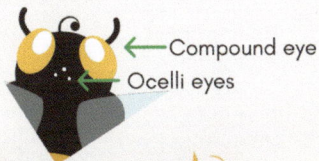

Compound eye

Ocelli eyes

Proboscis: The proboscis is part of the honey bee mouth. Honey bees use their proboscis to drink the nectar from flowers, honey, drink water, or sip any other liquids.

Abdomen: The abdomen is the part of the body where their legs and wings are attached.

Wings: Honey bees have 4 wings. They use their wings to fly.

Legs: Honey bees have 6 legs. They use their legs for walking. The workers bees have special parts on their legs to help them collect and carry pollen.

Stinger: The sting is a sharp organ that looks like a needle. It is located at the end of the bee's abdomen, and it is used to inject venom.

Did you know that the worker honey bees have a pollen basket on their legs?
They collect the pollen in the pollen basket and carry it back to the hive.

TYPE OF HONEY BEES AND THEIR JOBS

Queen bee: The queen bee is the star of the hive. She is responsible for laying eggs.

Drone bees: The drone bees are the male honey bees. The drone bees are the dads of the colony. They also help keep the hive cool by flapping their wings during the hot months.

Worker bees: The worker bees have many jobs. The young worker bees are the hive nurses, nurturing and feeding bee larvae. They also process the nectar, feed the queen, and make the honey. The older worker bees are the ones that look for food like nectar and pollen.

5 FUN FACTS ABOUT HONEY BEES

1 Drone honey bees do not have stingers.

2 Honey bees have 5 eyes! 2 large compound eyes and 3 smaller ocelli eyes in the center of their head.

3 A honey bee can visit between 50 to 100 flowers in one trip to collect nectar and pollen.

4 There can be 20,000 to 80,000 bees living in a colony.

5 A queen bee lives 2 to 3 years, but some could live up to 5 years!

GLOSSARY

Colony: A group of people who come from the same country, or animals of the same type living closely together like honey bees.

Emerge: Rise up from or come into view. Like a honey bee coming out of the honeycomb cell.

Metamorphosis: Changes in the form or parts of some animals as they grow. Metamorphosis occurs in animals like amphibians, insects, and some fish. For example, when a tadpole changes into a frog and a caterpillar change into a butterfly.

Transform: Change the form, look, or shape.

AMELIA LOCKHART

Printed in Great Britain
by Amazon

43928136R00016